Facilitator's Guide

Christian Disciplines

CREATING TIME AND SPACE FOR GOD

BEACON HILL PRESS
OF KANSAS CITY

Christian Disciplines

CREATING TIME AND SPACE FOR GOD

Writer/Editor
Mike L. Wonch
Director of Curriculum
Merritt J. Nielson
Director of Editorial
Bonnie Perry

ISBN: 978-0-8341-2986-3
Printed in U.S.A.

10 9 8 7 6 5 4 3 2 1

TABLE OF CONTENTS

USING THIS FACILITATOR'S GUIDE

The purpose of this facilitator's guide is to help you lead people into community as they grow in Christ by studying the Word.

TAKE A LOOK

1. Before you begin to prepare for the first session, get an overview of the entire study. This will enable you to:
    - Understand the direction of each session and the overall purpose of the study.
    - Know what your group will be reading and studying each week.
    - Begin to think and plan what you would like to accomplish by doing this study.
2. Before you teach each session,
    - Read over your Facilitator's Guide session for that week, several times, prior to your small group meeting. This will help you become familiar with questions, activities, options, and so on.
    - Gather any needed materials.
    - Pray for God's direction.

THE SESSIONS

Each session contains:

- *Opening our Minds*—the introductory material relevant to the topic for the session.
- *Opening the Word*—the Bible study portion of the session.
- *Opening our Hearts*—the opportunity for the group to understand how the truth discovered during the session applies to their lives.
- *Imaginative Option*—an activity option to bring extra creativity to your session.
- *Connect*—each week you will have the opportunity to send your class a text and/or email update of what you will study in the upcoming

week. We have provided the weekly text for you to use each week and is designed to be sent to your group the week prior to the session. You can use the message provided as is, or feel free to edit and add your own words to meet the needs of your particular group.

INVOLVE EVERYONE

We design the questions and activities to enable everyone to participate. Here are some things to keep in mind as you lead your small group:

1. Adults are more interested when they are participants instead of spectators.
2. They'll remember more of what they discuss and do together than what is said in a lecture.
3. When participants get involved in a discussion, be affirming and encouraging.
4. Don't force anyone to participate, but do make sure everyone knows his or her input is welcome.
5. Relax. Do your homework and don't feel tense about the session. Give your best effort, and let the Lord take care of the rest.
6. Pray for each adult in the session that they will benefit from the study. Pray for yourself that God will assist you as you lead.

ENCOURAGE GROUP MEMBERS . . .

- *To read.* Invite them to read the participant material prior to each session. This allows them to prepare their minds for the topic to be discussed that week.
- *To pray.* This allows them to prepare their hearts for what God wants to show them through the lesson.
- *To be open.* Be open to the lesson, the group members, and especially to God's leading.

SESSION 1

WHY DISCIPLINES?

Focus Scriptures: 1 Corinthians 9:24-27; Philippians 3:12-14

Session Goal: To understand that the Christian disciplines contribute to the transformation of heart and life, opening ourselves up to an increased capacity to love God and others.

OPENING OUR MINDS

Option 1

Begin by asking your group to imagine their goal is to become an Olympic competitor. They are to think of one specific event they would like to compete in (running, gymnastics, basketball, and so on). Ask them to consider what would be involved in becoming an Olympic athlete. Follow up by asking,

- **Can anyone show up to the Olympics and compete? Why, or why not?**
- **What do you think it takes to become an Olympian?**
- **Do you think training is involved? Explain.**
- **Do you think discipline is involved? Explain.**
- **What other areas of life do you think require training and discipline?**

Now, ask your group to think about the Christian life.

- **In what ways are training and discipline important to our relationship with God?**

Option 2

Divide your group into pairs. Share with the group that you are going to do some role playing. In each pair, one person will play the role of a new Christian and the other person will play the role of a mature Christian. Each pair is to role play a discussion as if the new Christian has asked the mature Christian, "What are the ways a person can grow in his or her relationship with God?" Allow time for discussion. Then, ask the pairs to switch roles. Follow up by asking the pairs to share what they discussed during this experience.

Imaginative Option

There are hundreds (maybe thousands) of exercise DVDs on the market today. These programs can range from fairly easy to extremely intense. Find a workout DVD and play a short segment. Then, ask the group to discuss how and why a person might use this type of workout.

- **Why is discipline important to being successful at this type of program?**
- **What kind of transformation takes place if a person is dedicated to this type of program?**

OPENING THE WORD

Understanding 1 Corinthians 9:24–27

In the verses prior to these, Paul encouraged believers to give up their rights, consider others first, bring people to Christ, to deny themselves, and look forward to the future. He compares the Christian life to running a race. The Olympics would have been in place during Paul's time. Then, as now, the athlete would need to train and prepare for participation in the games. The athlete trains for a crown that won't last forever. However, the Christian trains for a crown that lasts for eternity.

As believers, we do not train for competition against other believers. We train for the ultimate goal—eternal life with God. We discipline ourselves so that we stay "in shape" in our walk with God. These passages are a good example of the importance of maturing spiritually each day, from the time we accept Christ until we meet Him face-to-face.

Understanding Philippians 3:12–14

Paul understood that the Christian life was like a race that isn't complete until our lives on earth are over. He said that we must forget what's behind and press forward toward the goal—eternal life with God. God's calling on each life is to follow Him, daily surrendering our lives to His leading.

Option 1

Display an image of runners participating in a race for everyone in your group to see. Invite the group to take a few moments to think about the image. Then, ask the group what thoughts and feelings came to mind when they looked at the race imagery.

Read 1 Corinthians 9:24-27.

- **How is the Christian life like running a race?**
- **What kind of training does a runner participate in to get ready for a race? Why is this training important?**
- **What kind of "training" must we do as Christians? Why is this training important?**
- **Why is discipline an important part of our Christian growth?**
- **In terms of earning a prize/crown, what is the difference between a runner in a race and the Christian life?**

Read Philippians 3:12-14.

- **Why do you think Paul said he hadn't "arrived" at his "goal"? What goal do you think he was talking about?**
- **Why is it important to "forget what's behind" and to "strain toward what is ahead"?**
- **What does it mean to "press toward the goal" in our Christian walk?**

Option 2

Begin by writing the words "training" and "discipline" on a dry erase board. Ask the group how they would define each word, and write these next to the word. Then, ask them to think about someone who has made it their goal to run in a marathon.

- **How would "training" and "discipline" be important to help this runner achieve his or her goal of running and winning a race?**

Read 1 Corinthians 9:24-27 and Philippians 3:12-14.

- **How is the Christian life like a runner preparing for and competing in a race?**
- **How is the Christian life like a marathon rather than a sprint?**
- **What kind of "training" and "discipline" is necessary for us to grow in our walk with God?**
- **Why is it crucial for us to forget what's behind and to look forward?**
- **What is the ultimate goal/prize of every Christian?**

OPENING OUR HEARTS

Option 1

John Wesley referred to practices where we encounter God and cooperate with the Holy Spirit for the sake of increased capacity to love as "means of grace." Today, they are most often called "spiritual disciplines." Both terms communicate something important—the ultimate significance and goal of the practices are found in God's grace, but they require discipline on our part.

Share with the group the following in regard to the importance of Christian disciplines:

1. **We need to cooperate with God in order to grow spiritually.** Growth comes through an ongoing, lifelong relationship with God wherein we cooperate with the work of the Holy Spirit in the midst of our ordinary, daily lives.
2. **Being formed into Christlikeness takes time and patience.** When we receive Jesus into our lives we do not automatically become like Jesus. The disciplines keep us connected to God in this relationship, forming and shaping us into Christlikeness over the long haul.
3. **Spiritual growth takes place in the concrete.** Loving God and loving our neighbor take shape in the concrete practices of ordinary, human life and in and through our very human flesh-and-blood bodies. Disciplines are necessary in the Christian life because bodies require discipline to serve purposes higher than mere self-fulfillment.

In the weeks to come you will be looking at the disciplines of reading, praying, connecting, fasting, giving, and receiving. Ask,

- **What practices have you found helpful to your growth as a Christian?**
- **In what ways can we open our lives up to the leading of the Holy Spirit?**
- **Thinking silently to yourself: what is one thing you would like to see happen in your walk with God during this study?**

Close in prayer.

Imaginative Option

Bring items that a runner would use in preparation for a race. These might include shoes, jump rope, weights, and so on. Put these on a table and talk about how each of these items help a runner train for a race. Then, discuss those things necessary to help Christians in their walk with God.

Connect

WEEK 1

Why Disciplines?

THIS WEEK: Just as a runner is disciplined and trains for a race, we too, as Christians, must train and be disciplined in order to grow in our relationship with God. John Wesley referred to practices where we encounter God and cooperate with the Holy Spirit for the sake of increased capacity to love as the "means of grace." Today, they are most often called "spiritual disciplines." This week we will look at why the disciplines are important to our Christian walk.

THINK ABOUT THIS: What practices have you found helpful to your growth as a Christian?

PRAYER CONCERNS:

SESSION 2

READING: SHAPING STORY AND ENABLING PERSPECTIVE

Focus Scriptures: Psalm 119:97-105; 2 Timothy 3:14-17

Session Goal: To understand that reading the Bible is an indispensable practice for Christians. It is God's story that will re-shape and transform your personal story, your family story, and your national story.

OPENING OUR MINDS

Option 1

Begin by asking your group to call out famous/popular books, newspapers, or magazines. Ask,

- **Why do people read books? Newspapers? Magazines?**
- **In what ways do the things we read have an influence on us?**
- **Is there a difference between reading something for transformation and reading something for enjoyment? Explain.**

Option 2

Invite volunteers to share about a book they have read that made a difference in their lives (besides the Bible). Be sure to encourage them to include why they read the book and the ways this book impacted their life and why. After allowing as many as would like to share, ask,

- **What is the difference between reading a book that is fiction and one that is non-fiction?**
- **What is the difference between reading something for transformation and reading something for pure enjoyment?**
- **How does reading influence and impact your life?**
- **Are there any books that you can think of that have had an impact on the world? If so, why was this book so impactful?**

Imaginative Option

Bring in different types of books, including the Bible. These might include fiction, self-help, culinary, religious, and so on. Hold each book up and ask the group why people would read that type of book and how it might influence the person reading it. Then, hold up a Bible and ask the group why they believe people read the Bible and how it makes a difference in the lives of those who read it. Follow up by asking the group what sets the Bible apart from all other books.

OPENING THE WORD

Understanding Psalm 119:97-105

The psalmist, David, proclaimed his love for God's revelation to humankind. In fact he meditated on it all day. He found benefit in God's teaching and follows His instruction to guide him in a deeper understanding of God and His laws. As the psalmist obeyed God's Word, it became a "lamp" and "light" that led his path toward God and away from evil.

Understanding 2 Timothy 3:14-17

Timothy was dealing with false teachers in the church. Paul instructs Timothy to hold on to what he has learned from the Scriptures. Although he would have only had the Old Testament, his understanding and faith in Christ would have made the Scriptures more comprehensible—as it points to the Messiah.

The Holy Scriptures are God-breathed (inspired by God) and useful/profitable for teaching truth, rebuking those in sin, aiding people in correcting errors, and showing people how to live in righteousness. The study of God's Word is not just for knowledge, but to equip the believer to live out their faith in God.

Option 1

Write the word "Bible" on a dry erase board. Invite your group to say things that come to mind when they hear this word and write these on the board.

- **How do those who follow God view the Bible?**
- **How do you think non-believers view the Bible?**

Read Psalm 119:97-105.

- **From the verses read, how do you think the psalmist viewed God's Word?**
- **In what ways did the psalmist see God's Word profiting his life?**
- **How would you interpret the meaning of verse 103?**
- **How is God's Word a "light" and "lamp" to our path?**

Read 2 Timothy 3:14-17.

- **From the verses read, how do you think Paul viewed God's Word?**
- **In what ways did Paul see God's Word profiting a person's life?**
- **According to verse 16, how is God's Word useful/profitable to those who read it?**
- **How does the Bible equip us as believers?**

Option 2

Divide your group in half. Assign one group to read 119:97-105 and the other group to read 2 Timothy 3:14-17. Ask each group to discuss the following questions:

- **How does the writer view God's Word?**
- **List all the words used to describe God's Word?**
- **What is the benefit of God's Word to those who read it?**

Allow sufficient time for discussion. Then bring the groups together. Ask,

- **What did you discover about God's Word?**
- **Why is reading God's Word important for both the believer and the non-believer?**

OPENING OUR HEARTS

Option 1

Ask your group the following questions,

- **What are the biggest challenges to reading God's Word?**
- **How can we overcome these challenges?**

Because everyone is different, there are no "one-size-fits-all" steps to reading God's Word. However, share with your group some suggested ways to make reading God's Word a daily discipline in a person's life.

1. *Set aside time each day for reading.* This might be in the morning or at night. The key is to keep this time consistent.
2. *Pray for God's leading and direction before you read.* Allow God's presence to guide your thoughts.
3. *Don't be in a hurry.* Read the passage several times if needed. Allow time for reflection.
4. *Look for life application.* Ask God to show how the words apply to your life.
5. *End your time with prayer.* Invite God's Word to infiltrate every area of your life.

Option 2

Share with the group that reading the Bible gives us a new perspective—God's. The Bible can enable you to see yourself, your family, your ethnic group, and your nation from the perspective of God. Reading God's Word helps us understand the story of God and our place within that story.

- **In what ways does God's story in Scripture affect your life story?**
- **How can we incorporate God's Word into our lives this week?**

Invite your group to silently reflect on the Bible. Ask them to think about how they integrate reading God's Word into their daily schedule.

Imaginative Option

Distribute a 3x5 card to each person. Ask the group members to write the following on their card: *Time*, *Place*, and *Book*. Encourage the group to think about a time and place where they can daily read the Bible and write this on the card. Also, have them think of a book of the Bible that they can read and write this on the card. Urge group members to use this card as a daily reminder to read God's Word.

Connect

WEEK 2

Reading: Shaping Story and Enabling Perspective

THIS WEEK: Reading the Bible is an essential practice for Christians. It is God's story that will re-shape and transform your personal story, your family story, and your national story. This week we will examine the importance of reading God's Word in the life of His followers.

THINK ABOUT THIS: In what ways do I incorporate God's Word into my daily life?

PRAYER CONCERNS:

SESSION 3

PRAYING: SHAPING SPEECH AND ENABLING HONESTY

Focus Scriptures: Luke 11:1-13

Session Goal: To understand the importance of prayer as a daily discipline in our lives.

OPENING OUR MINDS

Option 1

Invite your group to respond to the following question: *What are the ways you communicate with . . .*

Parents

Spouse

Children

Friends

Coworkers

God

- **Why is communication important to any relationship?**
- **How is prayer an integral part of our relationship with God?**

Option 2

Ask your group how they would complete the following sentence: *Prayer is . . .*

Follow up by asking,

- **Why is it important for us to pray?**
- **Is there more than one way we can pray? If not, why?**
- **What are some misconceptions regarding prayer?**
- **What do you find most difficult or challenging about responding to God in prayer?**

Imaginative Option

Find items (or images) that people use to communicate with others. These might include a phone, pen and paper, traffic sign, and so on. Ask people how each item is used to communicate.

- **What makes communication important?**
- **In what ways do we communicate with God? In what ways does God communicate with us?**

OPENING THE WORD

Understanding Luke 11:1-13

We see prayer highlighted many times in the book of Luke (1:9-10; 3:21; 6:12; 9:18, 28-29). In today's passage, Jesus was asked about prayer by His disciples. In these 13 verses Jesus taught His disciples about the importance of prayer.

Jesus prayed, and so should His followers. We are to come to the Father asking, seeking, and knocking. God is listening and will answer. This does not mean that prayer is used to get God to give us whatever we want and ask. We must ask according to His will and follow the model Jesus has set before us. Following the example of Jesus, we must make time each day to pray to the Father.

Option 1

Read the following prayer to your group: "God is good. God is great. Let us thank Him for our food. Amen." Follow up by asking the group,

- **What kind of prayer is this?**
- **What is the focus of this prayer?**
- **Are there other standard prayers we use? If so, what are they?**

Read Luke 11:1-4.

- **Why do you think Jesus used this as a model for "how to pray"?**
- **What ideas are expressed in this prayer?**
- **Do you think this is the only way we are to pray? Why or why not?**

Read verses 5-10.

- **What do these verses say about our part in prayer?**
- **Why is asking, seeking, and knocking important to our prayers?**

- **Does this mean that God will answer the exact way we want Him to? Why or why not?**
- **How would you summarize these verses?**

Read verses 11-13.

- **What do these verses say about God?**
- **How would you summarize these verses?**

Option 2

Divide your group in half. Assign one group Luke 11:1-4 and the other group Luke 11:5-13. Give each group a piece paper and pen/pencil. Instruct each group to read their verses and then re-write the verses in modern-day language. Allow sufficient time. Then, bring the groups together and ask each group to share their discussion. Follow up by asking,

- **What do these verses say about our role in prayer?**
- **What do these verses say about God's role in prayer?**
- **What is the overall message, or messages, of these verses?**

OPENING OUR HEARTS

Option 1

While it would be shocking if there would be some in your group who have never prayed, many may not understand the different ways a person can pray. Remind the group that no matter when, where, or how they pray, prayer is two-way communication. That is to say, that we must always listen for God to speak to us as much (if not more) as we speak to God. Share with the group the following ways they can integrate prayer into their daily lives.

- **Praying the Scriptures**—Take a portion of Scripture and read it as a prayer to God. A good place to begin is the book of Psalms.
- **Formal prayers**—This is the time you set aside for personal and intercessory prayer.

- **Informal prayers**—These are prayers breathed as things come to your mind and you feel the need to pray.
- **Written prayers**—These are prayers that have been written by others that you read as your prayer to God.
- **Music**—Playing music and incorporating its words and message into your prayer to God.

There are many ways to pray. These are just some of the ways to help your group make prayer a daily discipline in their walk with God. Encourage your group to use one, or more, of the prayer practices mentioned above this week.

Option 2

Share with the group the following acrostic (A.C.T.S.) that can help group members develop a steady and defined prayer life.

- **A**doration—We begin by giving Him praise for being a great God and acknowledging His supremacy.
- **C**onfession—We acknowledge those things in our lives where we fall short of God's best for us and confess them, asking for forgiveness.
- **T**hanksgiving—We thank Him for all He has done, is doing, and will do in our lives.
- **S**upplication—We bring our requests and concerns before God.

While there is no formula for prayer, using these components may help guide group members as they begin to incorporate the discipline of prayer into their lives. Close by using the A.C.T.S. prayer blueprint.

Imaginative Option

Chris Tomlin has a song entitled "Lord I Need You." Invite your group to get quiet before God as this song plays. You may consider making a copy of the lyrics available to each person as the song is played. Close your time together in conversational prayer. This is the type of prayer where group members talk to God in the way they would talk to a friend. As you pray, anyone who feels led, is to breathe a sentence prayer out loud.

Connect

WEEK 3

Praying: Shaping Speech and Enabling Honesty

THIS WEEK: Prayer is communication offered to God in response to God's speaking to us. Prayer begins—not with us, but with God. God prays in us; as we join in, the praying becomes ours as well. This week we will see how to incorporate prayer into our daily lives.

THINK ABOUT THIS: How is prayer two-way communication with God?

PRAYER CONCERNS:

SESSION 4

CONNECTING: SHAPING VISION AND ENABLING HUMILITY

Focus Scriptures: Matthew 28:19-20; Ephesians 4:1-16

Session Goal: To understand how being connected to others is an important part of our Christian life.

OPENING OUR MINDS

Option 1

John Donne (1572-1631) was a poet and clergyman and one of the most influential poets of the Renaissance period. Read his poem, "No Man Is An Island," and ask the group what message they feel the poet is trying to convey. (You may consider giving each person a copy of the words.)

No man is an island,
Entire of itself.
Each is a piece of the continent,
A part of the main.
If a clod be washed away by the sea,
Europe is the less.
As well as if a promontory were.
As well as if a manor of thine own
Or of thine friend's were.
Each man's death diminishes me,
For I am involved in mankind.
Therefore, send not to know
For whom the bell tolls,
It tolls for thee.
—Meditation XVII, 1624

- **Why did God create each of us to be in relationship with others?**
- **Why are relationships important?**

Option 2

Invite your group to think about people they are connected to in their lives. These could be relatives, co-workers, friends, and so on. Allow time for some reflection. Then ask,

- **What makes each of these relationships different?**
- **What are the similarities in these relationships?**
- **How do you stay connected to these people?**
- **What are the barriers to expanding our circle of connection to others?**

Share with the group that it can be easier to connect with those who are like us, who like us, and who can advance our personal agendas, than it is to expand our circles to include those *not* like us, those who do *not* like us, and with whom relationship will *not* likely advantage us. However, expanding our circles of interaction to include "others" increases our capacity for loving God and neighbor.

Imaginative Option

Consider this exercise in "connecting." Divide your group into pairs. Ask each pair to take 30 seconds each to share three things about themselves with the other person. After a minute, change the pairs up. Continue this until each person has shared with every group member.

OPENING THE WORD

Understanding Matthew 28:19–20

Jesus, by His authority, commissioned His followers to go and make disciples as they preached the gospel, taught, and baptized. They were to reach out to others with the "good news" of Jesus. A disciple is to learn from the Master (Jesus), and in turn shares the message of the Teacher with others leading them toward a relationship with the Master (Jesus).

The disciples were to go to "all nations," not limiting this commission to just their small circle of friends or acquaintances. Today, we are to follow the Great Commission and reach out to the world, our world, with the message of Christ.

Understanding Ephesians 4:1–16

Paul had taught the church at Ephesus that Jews and Gentiles had been brought together in the faith. He then gave them instruction on how to exist and work together in unity. This unity comes through the Spirit as they worked together reaching harmony in the "faith and in the knowledge of the Son of God" becoming mature in their relationship with Christ.

All the parts of the body, with Christ, must stay connected and work together in order to be the people God has called us to be—the Church. No lone rangers. As Paul says, "From him the whole body, joined and held together by every supporting ligament, grows and builds itself up in love, as each part does its work."

Option 1

Begin by asking your group two questions:

- **What are the ways Christians connect with people outside the church?**
- **What are the ways Christians connect with one another inside the church?**

Read Matthew 28:19-20. Then, read it again. This time, as it is being read, invite the group to think about the ways this passage talks about believers' relationships with those in the world.

- **What do you think Jesus meant by telling the disciples to "go and make disciples"? How would you define "go" and "make"?**
- **How would you define "all nations"?**
- **What is the significance of "baptism"?**
- **Give examples of what "teaching" might look like in today's world?**
- **What do these verses say about the way Christians are to connect with those outside the church (non-believers)?**

Read Ephesians 4:1-16. Then, read it again. This time as it is being read invite the group to think about the ways this passage talks about believers' relationships to other believers.

- **Why are being humble, gentle, and bearing with one another in love crucial to healthy relationships?**
- **How are peace and unity tied together?**
- **Considering each person is created unique, how do we use our uniqueness, gifts, and abilities to function as the body of Christ (with Christ as the head of the body)?**
- **Why is maturity important to healthy relationships?**
- **What do these verses say about the way Christians are to connect with other believers?**

Option 2

Ask for a volunteer to share a story of how connecting with a non-believer helped he or she grow as a Christian. Then, read Matthew 28:19-20.

- **What do these verses say about the ways we are to connect with those outside the Church?**

Ask for another volunteer to share a story of how connecting with a believer helped he or she grow as a Christian. Then, read Ephesians 4:1-16.

- **What do these verses say about the ways we are to connect with those inside the Church?**

Invite the group to think about the message of both scripture passages. (You may consider reading them again.)

- **In what ways is connecting with those outside the church different from connecting with those inside the church? How are they similar?**
- **What is the message of Matthew 28:19-20 and Ephesians 4:1-16?**

OPENING OUR HEARTS

Option 1

Share with the group that as Christ-followers we are to connect with those inside the church as well as those outside the church. The discipline of connecting means that we continually expand our circle of interaction with others. Discuss the following ways to connect with others.

- **Local body of Christ**. Christian worship is most spiritually formative when the gathering expands your circle of interaction beyond your individual self.
- **Accountability groups**. Regularly meeting with a small group or one-to-one with a spiritual mentor provides the right mix of companionship and challenge for growth in holiness.

- **Christian groups**. Fellowship and cooperation between differing Christian groups increases your capacity to love others, thereby equipping you for interaction with non-Christians.
- **Community and workplace**. It takes discipline to prayerfully and intentionally connect and share Jesus with people who may have a different skin color, speak a different language, live on the other side of town (especially if it has a reputation as a place to avoid), or practice a different religion (or no religion at all).
- **Globally.** You will be made (spiritually formed) into a more mature disciple when you connect with others who live in worlds beyond your borders, whether they are local, regional, national, ethnic, economic, or religious borders.
- **Your enemies**. Only by connecting with your enemies, not to fight them but to seek their well-being, can you learn how to forgive—the hallmark of the Gospel message.

Connect

WEEK 4

Connecting: Shaping Vision and Enabling Humility

THIS WEEK: Expanding our circles of connection becomes the laboratory wherein God expands our capacity to love, not only our neighbor, but God too. This week we will see how the connection between love of God and love of human beings is a necessary one.

THINK ABOUT THIS: If the Good Samaritan parable were to be re-told in your context, what people group(s) might substitute for "Samaritan"?

PRAYER CONCERNS:

SESSION

5

FASTING: SHAPING APPETITE AND ENABLING SELF-CONTROL

Focus Scriptures: Isaiah 58:1-9; Matthew 6:16-18

Session Goal: To understand what fasting is and its importance to the Christian life.

OPENING OUR MINDS

Option 1

Invite your group to respond to the following statements about fasting. You may get a mixed response, so allow the group time to share their opinions.

Fasting is a public display of your spirituality.

Fasting is way to remind yourself that life is more than physical nourishment.

Fasting is for everybody.

Fasting makes us more spiritual.

Fasting is a great way to lose weight.

Fasting is an opportunity to recognize God's work in your life.

Option 2

Give each person a slip of paper and pencil/pen. Ask each group to complete the sentence *Fasting is . . .* by writing it on their slip of paper. Once everyone has finished, collect the slips and put them in a container. Mix them up. Then, one at a time, read each slip.

- **Do you think most people understand the purpose and practice of fasting? Why, or why not?**
- **What is the most difficult thing to understand about fasting?**
- **Do you think most Christians fast often, rarely, or not at all?**

Imaginative Option

Take a paper plate and write the word "Fasting" in the middle with a marker. Then, hand the plate and marker to a group member and invite him or her to write one word on the plate that comes to mind regarding fasting. When he or she finishes, have this person pass it to someone else. Repeat this process until everyone in the group has had a chance to write something.

Follow up by reading all the responses written on the plate. Consider asking for several volunteers who have fasted to share their experience with the group.

OPENING THE WORD

Understanding Isaiah 58:1-9

God called upon Isaiah to deliver a message to the Israelites. The people looked spiritual and religious, but God looked into their hearts and saw self-serving actions. They seemed religious while at the same time exploited their workers. Even while fasting they were quarreling and brawling. The message from God was clear: acts of religiousness are not just something we do, but are done out of a heart of sincere faith. Fasting was not a sacred performance, but was to result in acts of justice and mercy toward others.

Understanding Matthew 6:16–18

Fasting was mandatory once a year for the Jewish people, during the Day of Atonement. However, people or groups could fast for certain petitions made to God. During the time of Jesus, the Pharisees fasted twice a week and had turned the practice into a way to get the public's support. Jesus reminded the disciples that they should not fast in a way that draws attention to themselves, but should be done quietly and sincerely before God. Fasting is not a matter of public display and gaining the respect of others; it is to be done with the purpose of drawing closer to the Father.

Option 1

Read Isaiah 58:1-5.

Share with the group that Isaiah spoke a word from God to the Israelites. They thought the *act* of fasting was what mattered. They failed to see that attitude was the key. Spiritual disciplines are more about the heart and mind than about the body in action.

- **What was the prophet's message to the people?**
- **In what ways had the people disregarded God's commands?**

Read verses 6-9.

- **What sort of fasting does God desire?**
- **How should fasting make a difference in our relationship with God? With others?**

Read Matthew 6:16-18.

- **How do you think the "hypocrites" viewed fasting? What was their motivation?**
- **In what way had they already received their reward?**
- **According to Jesus, what is the way we should fast?**
- **What reward do you think we receive when we fast the way Jesus taught?**
- **How is the approach to fasting for hypocrites different from those who fast as Jesus taught?**
- **Why do you think fasting is a private act rather than a public act?**

Option 2

Divide your group in half. Assign one group Isaiah 58:1-9 and the other group Matthew 6:16-18. Give each group a piece of paper and pen/pencil. Instruct each group to read their passage and write the message these verses contain regarding fasting. Allow sufficient time for groups to read and discuss. Then, bring everyone together and ask each group to share their findings.

OPENING OUR HEARTS

Option 1

Share with your group that fasting is denying yourself something that is good. It acknowledges the goodness of that which is denied—food, drink, sex, entertainment, information, power—and reinforces that goodness by refusing to serve it as a god. Fasting reaffirms God as the ultimate Good Creator and Provider.

- **What can fasting symbolize?** (Self-denial, dependence on God, drawing closer to God, subservience of earthly appetites to our walk with God, practice in self-control, and so on.)
- **How do we know when it is time to fast?** (Spiritual hunger, self-control issues, problems, and so on.)
- **How does prayer play a vital role in the practice of fasting?**

Close by asking your group to seek God's guidance in the spiritual discipline of fasting.

Option 2

If God is leading you to fast, consider these practical suggestions:

1. *Classify your appetites.* What are your greatest natural appetites (food, drink, power, media distraction, spending)? Which of these do you have the least self-control? Which of these, when catered to, tend to weaken your desire for God and God's work in the world? Make these the starting place for your fasting practice.
2. *Examine your motives.* Christian disciplines can be practiced for the wrong reasons. Keep the focus on loving God and entering more into God's mission in the world.
3. *Start small.* Keep your discipline brief and non-strenuous, so that you can listen carefully to your body and gradually adjust the routine so that it strengthens rather than harms you.

4. *Do it for the sake of others.* When you fast from food, remember those who are continually hungry. When you fast from spending money, remember those who do not have adequate financial resources. Go a step further: combine your fast with acts of charity and work for justice.
5. *Link it with prayer and accountability.* The Scriptures almost always link fasting with praying (Mark 9:29), and for good reason. It is not a discipline to be practiced alone. Acknowledge God at the beginning and end, thank God for the gifts of life, intercede for others who are suffering and in need, and ask God to use your self-denial to make you more Christlike.

Close by asking your group to seek God's guidance in the spiritual discipline of fasting.

Connect

WEEK 5

Fasting: Shaping Appetite and Enabling Self-Control

THIS WEEK: All of the Christian disciplines help move us beyond just living for ourselves. This week we will see how fasting helps us in that it challenges self-serving love at the most basic level of our bodily appetites.

THINK ABOUT THIS: Are there things in your life where you lack self-control?

PRAYER CONCERNS:

SESSION 6

GIVING: SHAPING ATTITUDE AND ENABLING GENEROSITY

Focus Scriptures: 2 Corinthians 9:6-15

Session Goal: To understand how to incorporate the spiritual discipline of giving into our daily lives.

OPENING OUR MINDS

Option 1

- Invite several volunteers to share a time when someone was generous to them. How did this make them feel? What did they learn from this experience?
- Invite several volunteers to share a time when they were generous to someone. How did this make them feel? What did they learn from this experience?

Ask,

- **What are the benefits of someone being generous to us?**
- **What are the benefits to us being generous to others?**

Option 2

Generosity is defined as *"kindness: willingness to give money, help, or time freely."*[1]

- **How would you describe a generous person?**
- **How would you describe generosity to someone else?**
- **Is there a difference between worldly generosity and Christian generosity? If so, what?**

Imaginative Option

Show the clip from the movie "It's A Wonderful Life" where George Baily is surrounded by friends who are bringing money to help him in his time of crisis. This clip shows the generosity of his friends who are giving back to George in light of his generosity toward them. Follow-up by asking,

- **How did this clip show the act of generosity?**
- **Is this an accurate depiction of giving?**

1. http://www.bing.com/Dictionary/search?q=define+generosity&qpvt=generosity &FORM=DTPDIA. Accessed September 6, 2012.

OPENING THE WORD

Understanding 2 Corinthians 9:6-15

The Corinthian church had been very generous in the past. In fact, Paul had boasted to the Macedonians about their giving. Paul was ready to collect again, but the church may have been less enthusiastic about giving this time around. The apostle was worried that their donations may be "grudgingly given" (v. 5). He reminded them that God desires an eager and cheerful giver.

The amount of the gift takes a back seat to the attitude in which it is given. In Christ, God gave the greatest gift. God's generosity should motivate us to give all we can with a cheerful heart. Our generosity is a reflection of our thankfulness to God for all He has done for us!

Option 1

Divide everyone into groups of three. Give each group a print out of 2 Corinthians 9:6-15 and a highlighter. Ask each group to read the passage, then highlight and discuss anything that stands out to them from this passage. After sufficient time, bring the groups together. Invite each group to share what they highlighted and why. Follow up by asking,

- **What is the main message, or messages, of these verses?**
- **If someone were to ask you to explain the concept of a "cheerful giver," based on these passages, what would you say to this person?**

Option 2

Read 2 Corinthians 9:6-15. Share with the group that the Corinthian church had been generous in their giving in the past. The apostle Paul had even bragged to the Macedonians about how generous they had been. Paul was ready to collect again, but the church may have seemed less eager to give then they had been in the past. The apostle was concerned that they may be giving, but doing so grudgingly.

Read verses 6-9.

- **What do you think the phrase "whoever sows sparingly will also reap sparingly and whoever sows generously will also reap generously" means?**
- **Do you think God requires everyone to give the same amount? Why, or why not?**
- **What is the difference between a "cheerful giver" and one who gives "reluctantly" or "under compulsion"?**
- **How would you interpret verses 8-9?**

Read verses 10-16.

- **In what ways does God "supply and increase our store of seed", "enlarge the harvest of our righteousness", and "make us rich"?**
- **How does our giving result in thankfulness toward God?**
- **What is the gift God has given us? Can we ever repay that gift?**
- **What should be our attitude in our giving to others?**
- **How does giving impact our relationship with God? With others?**

OPENING OUR HEARTS

Option 1

Share with the group the following ways they can offer (give) to others as an authentic expression of their lives.

- **Your presence.** Just being with someone is a great gift to others.
- **Your time.** Making time for another says, "I care."
- **Your money and possessions.** You are a steward of the money and possessions God has blessed you with.
- **Your abilities.** It's not about what you can't do, but what you can do. Do what you can, as to the Lord (Romans 12:6-8).
- **Your testimony.** This means sharing your faith in Christ with someone else through words and actions.

Ask your group to silently reflect on the following question: **From the list above, what do you find it easiest to give? The hardest to give?** Follow up by asking your group to think about one way they can give to another this week.

Option 2

Take time to share with the group that John Wesley used the phrase *works of mercy* in reference to "giving actions" that form us in Christlikeness. These are actions aimed at serving others. Share these keys to giving to others.

- *Look at the needs of those around you.* Open your eyes to those who may need your generosity.
- *Set aside time to serve others.* Be intentional in your service to others.
- *Budget so to give of your financial resources.* Tithe and offerings.
- *Use your gifts and abilities.* Consider ways to utilize the gifts and abilities God has blessed you with.
- *Encourage others through words and actions.* Using the words you speak and the way you live as an encouragement to others.

Close by asking your group to think about one specific way they could give to others this week.

Imaginative Option

Bring a watch, a dollar bill, and a mirror to your group meeting. Pass the watch around and ask the group to think about one way they could give of their time this week. Then, pass the dollar bill around and ask the group to think of one way they could give of their financial resources this week. Finally, pass around the mirror and ask the group to think about one way they could give of themselves this week.

Connect

WEEK 6

Giving: Shaping Attitude and Enabling Generosity

THIS WEEK: Generosity takes on many forms. This week we will see how generous giving is both an attitude and a behavior. We see the proper *attitude* most clearly in Jesus "who, being in very nature God, did not consider equality with God something to be used to his own advantage;" and the corresponding proper *behavior*: "rather, he made himself nothing by taking the very nature of a servant" (Philippians 2:6-7).

THINK ABOUT THIS: In what ways can I give to others?

PRAYER CONCERNS:

SESSION 7

RECEIVING: SHAPING POSTURE AND ENABLING TRUST

Focus Scriptures: Colossians 3:1-17

Session Goal: To understand how the discipline of receiving helps us focus on our dependence on God's grace.

OPENING OUR MINDS

Option 1

Show a picture of a baby to your group. Ask the group to think about what is involved to ensure a baby grows in a healthy way. (These might include love, nutrition, medicine, and so on.) Then, show a picture of an adult. Ask the group to think about what is involved to ensure an adult continues to grow in a healthy way.

- **Why is growth necessary for a baby?**
- **Why is continued growth necessary for an adult?**
- **What would happen if a person decided to stop doing things necessary for growth?**
- **What is necessary for a person to grow in their relationship with God?**

Option 2

Invite your group to reflect on the following questions:

- **What are the ways you foster growth in your relationship with your spouse?**
- **What are the ways you foster growth in your relationship with your children?**
- **What are the ways you foster growth in your relationship with your friends?**
- **What are the ways you foster growth in your relationship with God?**
- **Why is growth necessary in our relationships?**

Imaginative Option

Before your group meets, find a CD that has prayerful worship music. Invite your group to bow their heads and close their eyes, getting quiet before God. Then, play the music at a medium to low volume. Ask the group to reflect on their relationship with God by considering the following questions:

- **I feel like my relationship with God is . . .**
- **I would like my relationship with God to be . . .**

OPENING THE WORD

Understanding Colossians 3:1-17

In chapter two of this letter to the church at Colossae, Paul addressed the issue of false teachers. Now he changes the focus to Christian conduct. When we accept Christ, we put on the new self and put to death the earthly nature. We are transformed by allowing Christ to live in us so that we may become what God intends us to be. As God's chosen people, we are to clothe ourselves in Christlikeness.

God calls His followers to a life of holiness. Through the Holy Spirit we are empowered to live and grow in our relationship with God as we daily surrender our lives to Him. Growth does not happen by accident; it comes through aligning our lives with God's and participating in those practices that draw us closer Him (i.e. prayer, fasting, reading the Word, and so on).

Option 1

Divide your group into pairs. Ask each pair to read Colossians 3:1-17 and discuss what the passage says and its message for us today. Allow sufficient time for discussion. Then, bring everyone together. Ask the group to freely share their discussion. Follow up by asking,

- **What is the message, or messages, of these verses?**
- **How would you summarize these passages in two or three sentences?**

Option 2

Share with the group that when we accept Christ we are "spiritual infants." We are born anew, from spiritual death to spiritual life in Christ. God does not want us to stay infants, but continue to grow in our relationship with Him. Read Colossians 3:1-17.

Read verses 1-4.

- **What does it mean for us to "set our minds on things above"? Why is that important?**
- **In what ways is Christ "our life"? (v. 4)**

Read verses 5-11.

- **How do we put to death those things that belong to our "earthly nature"?**
- **Why is it necessary to get rid of anger, rage, malice, slander, filthy language, and lying?**
- **What are the ways we "put on the new self"?**

Read verses 12-14.

- **How do we clothe ourselves with compassion, kindness, humility, gentleness, and patience?**
- **In what ways do forgiveness and love bring unity among believers?**

Read verses 15-17.

- **How do we incorporate the Word, psalms, and hymns into our daily walk with God? What else should we incorporate into our daily walk?**
- **Why is doing everything—our words and actions—in the name of Jesus important?**

OPENING OUR HEARTS

Option 1

The Christian life is not meant to be lived on our own strength. God has promised His Holy Spirit to give us power, guidance, and direction to live each day in Christlikenss. As followers of Christ, we must position ourselves in such a way as to receive God's grace. A key to our spiritual formation is receiving. Receiving from God helps us be open and remain open to God's leading, and pushes away our leaning toward self-sufficiency.

Ask your group to think about the Christian disciplines (reading, praying, connecting, fasting, giving, and receiving).

- **How does practicing disciplines open ourselves up to God's working in our lives?**
- **In what ways can we position ourselves to receive God's grace in our lives?**

Option 2

Share with your group that practicing the Christian discipline of receiving is about opening ourselves up to God's grace. Read the following prayer as a way to close your time together. You may consider printing copies for each person. Before you pray, invite group members to reflect on the ways they can open themselves up to God's grace and presence this week.

A Prayer of John Wesley:
"O that we may all receive of Christ's fullness, grace upon grace; grace to pardon our sins, and subdue our iniquities; to justify our persons and to sanctify our souls; and to complete that holy change, that renewal of our hearts, whereby we may be transformed into that blessed image wherein thou didst create us."

Imaginative Option

The Lord's Supper/Communion is a means of grace. That is way we acknowledge what Christ has done and as a testimony of our faith and relationship with God. This sacrament opens ourselves up to God's grace. Consider asking the pastor to come and serve Communion to your group.

Connect

WEEK 7

Receiving: Shaping Posture and Enabling Trust

THIS WEEK: This week we will look at the Christian discipline of receiving and how it opens us up to a dependency on God's grace. We will discover how the relational posture toward God most conducive to ongoing spiritual formation is receiving.

THINK ABOUT THIS: In what ways do you receive God's grace in your life?

PRAYER CONCERNS: